How To Stop Being Too Nice

The Ultimate Guide on How To Stop Being So Nice

Michael Emily & Patrick James

Table of Contents

Chapter 1

Perils of Being Too Nice

Being "nice" is something that is embedded in us from childhood; we are taught to serve others, be thoughtful, and kind in spirit. Showing compassion and kindness to those we encounter on a daily basis enriches both their and our lives.

It is critical to consider other people's feelings and avoid imposing one's own. Being respectful and knowing when to compromise improves life and makes things flow more smoothly. Making people happy usually makes us popular and easy to get along with.

Unfortunately, while we may believe that being everyone's go-to person is wonderful, there are some real drawbacks to being "too kind'. It can be detrimental to both your physical and emotional well-being. These people prefer to suppress negative feelings, such as anger and disappointment, which leads to irritation and resentment, which in the long run can lead to anxiety, depression, and addiction.

While compassion is unquestionably a virtue, most people have a limit to their giving. Unless you are one of those people who are labeled as "kind-hearted to a fault," which is not praise. Someone who always prioritizes the wants of others before their own and is constantly walked all over.

Recognizing the Disadvantages of Excessive Niceness

We sometimes associate kindness with weakness, and niceness is generally undervalued in the human interaction economy. There is a delicate line, muddied by society's expectations, between the virtue of kindness and the vice of self-effacement. With that, let's consider the everlasting disadvantages of being overly polite.

Being overlooked
The individual who cloaks himself in continual niceness frequently disappears into the background. He becomes an inconspicuous background character in a story dominated by people who take the stage. According to social

psychology research, assertive persons are more likely to be remembered and identified in group settings. A study published in the Journal of Personality and Social Psychology discovered that persons who speak up and express their ideas confidently are viewed as more competent and leadership-worthy.

Used as a doormat
History is not kind to those who let themselves be trampled on. The annals of time are rich with tales of men who, in their extreme generosity, became footnotes in their own lives.

Consider the psychological idea of 'learned helplessness', which occurs when a person believes they are unable to change a terrible circumstance as a result of repeated exposure to adversity. This phenomenon, investigated by psychologist Martin Seligman, reflects the dilemma of the extremely kind person.

A person who is accustomed to being used may develop a sense of impotence, similar to the tragic destiny of King Lear in Shakespeare's play. Today's too-nice man faces a similar destiny, with his compassion misinterpreted as weakness and his generosity abused by others who see a chance to profit from his unyielding desire to submit.

Lack of Respect
Assertiveness is frequently used to get respect. The man who walks in armed just with niceness is quickly disarmed. The too-nice man is thus forced to roam the margins of influence, his voice drowned out by the clamor of those who demand respect through a combination of compassion and strength.

According to a Harvard Business Review study, leaders who blend warmth and strength, the two components of respect, have the highest levels of team engagement and loyalty. The too-nice man, who provides warmth without counterbalancing strength, may find himself valued neither as a leader nor as a competitor.

Losing Your Identity
In the never-ending effort of pleasing others, a guy can lose sight of what makes him special. Each block of stone contains a statue, which the artist must discover. But the man who is too polite becomes a canvas for the whims of others around him, with his true personality serving as a mere undercoat.

The psychological word for this is self-concept confusion,' which is defined as a lack of clarity regarding one's own views and desires. According to a study published in the Journal of Clinical Psychology, this might lead to a loss of self-esteem and sadness. The too-pleasant man risks becoming a stranger to himself, his own passions and interests hidden beneath layers of other people's expectations.

Obsessed with approval

The desire for acceptance may be an unhealthy addiction. The overly pleasant man can get obsessed with the desire for external validation. This preoccupation is more than simply a personal crisis; it has been demonstrated to have a harmful impact on mental health.

According to social psychology research, a high demand for acceptance is associated with increased stress and decreased psychological well-being.

Mental exhaustion

The too-nice man's attempt to be always agreeable is a comparable exercise in futility, one that can lead to mental fatigue. According to the Journal of Experimental Psychology, cognitive overload is not merely a metaphor, but a clinically recognized syndrome that frequently results in decision fatigue and diminished cognitive resources. The too-nice man, in his over-analysis of every social contact, jeopardizes his mental health in pursuit of an unreachable level of niceness.

Seen as dull

The man who muffles his opinions and hides his personality behind agreeableness runs the risk of being labeled a dullard. This sense of dullness is not without consequences. According to a study published in the Personality and Social Psychology Bulletin, people who lack distinguishing characteristics are less likely to be remembered or have an impact.

Unmet needs

The too-nice man frequently finds himself in deprivation, his own needs unmet as he devotes his energy to others. It's a dynamic similar to self-neglect. The psychological study highlights this situation, demonstrating that continuous disregard of one's own needs in favor of others can lead to stress and decreased life satisfaction, according to the American Psychological Association's results.

Self-Sacrificing

Self-sacrifice has a noble edge, but when it becomes habitual, it turns into a blade that slashes the wielder. According to a study published in the American Journal of Health Promotion, this constant self-sacrifice is associated with lower personal well-being and may even lead to burnout. The too-nice man, in his desire to put everyone else first, may become a martyr of his own creation, his personal aspirations and wants sacrificed to meet the demands of others.

Time Drain

Time is the currency of life, and the guy who spends it all on others risks going bankrupt. This is more than just philosophical musing; it is a reality founded on the economic notion of opportunity cost. Every moment dedicated to another's cause detracts from one's own. The too-polite man, generous with his time, may not realize the cost until it's too late.

Avoiding Responsibilities

The too-nice individual, in his aversion to the uncomfortable, may end up on a similar road, where the obligations he avoids today become the problems he must face tomorrow. According to research in organizational behavior, workplace conflict avoidance can lead to larger issues later on, such as decreasing team performance and satisfaction.

Bullying Target

Niceness might attract bullies since it is perceived as submissive conduct. According to studies published in the Journal of Community & Applied Social Psychology, bullies are more likely to target persons who are non-confrontational and docile. In his hesitation to stand firm, the too-nice man may unintentionally paint a bullseye on his back, which bullies are all too eager to aim at.

Unattractiveness

In the laws of attraction, excessive niceness can be the mistake that costs the too-nice man the lead. It's a trait that, when exaggerated, implies a lack of assertiveness and confidence, which are frequently associated with magnetic charisma.

This phenomenon is represented in social psychologists' studies, which state that assertiveness is frequently associated with attractiveness. The too-nice man, in his zeal to please, may accidentally dull the very light that may attract others to him, his niceness obscuring the more compelling qualities of his character.

Loss of Personal Growth
The journey of the too-nice man is frequently one of stagnation, with little opportunity for personal development. It's a secure path, but it doesn't lead to much self-discovery or resilience building. The too-nice man deprives himself of the experiences that spur development and transformation because he is afraid of confrontation or challenge. According to developmental psychology research, encountering problems is important for human growth since it forces people to adapt, learn, and evolve.

The primary point is not to minimize the benefit of being pleasant but to acknowledge the significance of setting boundaries and striking a balance.

Chapter 2

Setting Boundaries

Boundaries are difficult for genuinely decent people. If you care deeply and have a lot of compassion, you probably see the best in everyone, so you can typically understand why someone is hurting and forgive their faults. You're probably giving too many opportunities to the wrong folks. Furthermore, you do not want to make someone feel awful. You're a very wonderful individual. If this is making you unhappy, as it undoubtedly does, here are some simple lessons to help you improve your habits.

Friendship is a gift
No one owes you their time, friendship, kindness, or help. You also do not owe anyone else these things. To feel entitled to love is to diminish the importance of a genuinely chosen friendship or partnership.

Sometimes a genuinely lovely person believes she can earn another person's affection by loving them hard enough. Perhaps she believes that if she tells others how they have harmed her or how much she has done for them, they will be forced to love her. Even if she is very sweet, these aren't ideal conditions for a romantic connection. The only valid premise for a relationship is mutual consent. Otherwise, it must leave.

Learning to gracefully let someone go is one of the most important signs of adulthood. It's always unfortunate when things don't work out, but people can pick who they want to be friends with and how much they want to be friends with at any time; people change, and life is long. The beauty is that our friendships should always make us feel appreciated and chosen.

To let people go gently, you must recognize that you are valuable and lovely, even if you are not everyone's cup of tea. It demands you improve your talent at pursuing friendships by inviting individuals to hang out and perform activities to get to know them better. It also requires you to remember the third rule: it's usually not about you. Perhaps the other individual is going through something. Maybe the time is off. Perhaps they have opted to shift their principles or culture. Let them go, persuade yourself that you're terrific, and call someone else!

Mental health

If you are lonely, mourning, anxious, or in pain, you must tackle your own problems, not those of others. That is not to say you are unlovable while coping with your troubles. Everybody has their own problems to handle. Understanding that you are the only one who can get your happiness back is vital. Your friends and family can be sad for you, support you, love you, and remind you of who you are. However, they cannot solve it for you. They cannot make the pain or anxiety go away.

They are not responsible for saving you from your unpleasant feelings or difficulties, and you should not expect them to behave in irrational ways to alleviate your anxiety or unhappiness; it is your responsibility, not theirs. Similarly, you should not try to solve other people's issues or devote all of your time and energy to finding someone else's happiness. Such expectations are not fair to anyone since they foster reliance and unequal power dynamics. Each of us must combat our own demons.

If I'm in a relationship where John is constantly trying to make me happy, and I'm always trying to make John happy, and we mostly connect because of underlying feelings like loneliness or pain, things will quickly become dishonest and confusing: no one is making honest decisions for their own well-being or clearly expressing their needs!

It is good to show affection to others. It is not desirable to sacrifice our own needs or happiness in order to meet the needs of others. We must be able to show love to others as part of expressing ourselves, rather than as a means of ignoring our own needs and desires.

Asking for what you want or saying what you need is an extremely crucial ability in this context. There's nothing heroic or humble about ignoring your own needs and letting them go because they don't. They simply fester, forming walls between you and others. If you do not initiate talks or communicate your feelings, you are burdening the other individual in the relationship by forcing them to guess. Worst case scenario, you're confusing people. Do not do that. It is your job to communicate your wants and needs. It is not another person's responsibility to figure them out.

Know what you possess

One of the most crucial aspects of a relationship is understanding what is yours and what is the other person's. Your anguish, sadness, and past are yours. How you treat or care for others is entirely up to you. Your habits, thoughts, and dreams are your own. Others, however, have their own desires, goals, pasts, comfort zones, choices, values, and lives. They have their own emotions.

Really lovely individuals struggle with this: how can I disagree with someone I care deeply about? How can I do anything that will make them upset? But it's vital to realize that others can be upset by things you say and do for yourself, and you can still do them. Neither you nor the other person should feel guilty about the behavior or reaction. In fact, if you simply allow them to be upset while remaining firm in your decision, the relationship will most likely survive. Usually, this only makes others appreciate you more.

It's also important to remember that the most hurtful things you'll ever experience were almost definitely not about you. Sometimes you will injure others in the same way. Yes, even the nicest individuals can damage others' sentiments.

The lovely thing about ownership is that when others show love to you, it is significant, and you must learn to wonder and accept it. Knowing what we own, what we control, and what others have done for us enables us to accept responsibility and feel grateful. It enables us to start meaningful conversations and convey our frustrations or needs.

When you understand what you own, you can say "sorry" if you did anything terrible to someone else. When you know what someone else has, you may say "thank you" when something nice comes from them. And these simple words are important.

People frequently use the term "boundaries" without understanding what a boundary is. Or they believe a boundary is a wall. Boundaries are personal understandings that enable us to love each other more. Just as two countries would be unable to cooperate effectively if they did not know where one's jurisdiction ended and the other's began, we require boundaries to determine whose problems are whose.

If John and Dora have healthy limits in their relationship, both will feel that it fits their needs and offers them happiness. Each person will feel free to communicate their diverse perspectives, valid sentiments, and needs. Even if one of them changed substantially or went away, each would have a strong feeling of their own identity and importance.

Walls are different. Walls form when we do not speak honestly, do not voice our own wants or make choices for our own pleasure, and allow resentment or hurt to accumulate between people.

If John and Dora have crossed their personal boundaries, they may be unsure whether their presence is important to the other person. They may value the feelings of others to the point where they lose sight of their own. They might not be honest about things that have hurt them. They may be hesitant to share their own opinions or live their own lives for fear of offending the other person or ending the relationship.

This condition will result in walls. Each individual must shield himself from the emotional pain caused by the relationship. Each individual will resist bringing their entire selves to the table. Most likely, each person will experience a great deal of hurt, pain, and resentment, but only in secret, behind a wall.

Boundaries establish a safe environment for trust. They are how people may disagree, be angry, hurt, and express their actual sentiments while still loving and laughing together. They are how individuals discover and experience their own happiness. Boundaries are necessary for successful relationships, and we can all learn to maintain them.

Chapter 3

Assertiveness Training

Some of the kindest individuals I know struggle to be forceful. And, yeah, looking out for number one and saying no when someone asks for too much might come seem selfish. However, if you define assertiveness as merely discussing and compromising, you may discover that it falls squarely within the purview of a good person. Nice people are used to pitching in and doing more than their fair part, and they are sensitive to the sentiments of others. When requested to help, you will most likely gladly volunteer. When asked to give, you do.

Every scenario and individual is unique, thus we need adaptable assertiveness. Everyone knows someone who is forceful, dominating, or aggressive. They appear to prioritize their own interests over those of others, and as a result, they have difficulty interacting with others. When asserting yourself in front of these folks, you must be firm and confident.

Others will profusely apologize for not being more insightful and fair if you simply express what you need or set your limits. Recognizing that assertiveness is not one-size-fits-all, let us look at some recommendations.

How To Be Forceful While Remaining Nice

Practice
Stop saying "I don't care" or "it doesn't matter to me" when people ask you what you want. Practice expressing your viewpoint on trivial matters. Practice asking for items to increase your comfort level. "Could you save my seat?" "Does anybody have an extra pen?" Practice saying "no" to people who want to cut in line in front of you.

Use "I" statements
Saying "I believe" or "I disagree" sounds less accusatory than saying "You're wrong" or "You must do your fair part of the work."

Concentrate on particular behavior rather than making it personal

If you disagree with something someone is doing, avoid making broad
generalizations about their character. Instead, concentrate on specific
behavior at a certain time.

Say "no"
If you don't want to do anything or don't have time, saying "no" is essential.
But it does not have to be blunt. "I'm grateful you thought of me for this, but I'll
be working with the conference all next week."

Have a consistent message
If you're dealing with someone who is manipulating, taking advantage of your
guilt, or being extremely aggressive, repeat your point clearly and as often as
necessary.

Do not be apologetic or self-effacing.
Avoid using phrases like "I'm sorry, but..." or "It might just be me, but..."
before making your case.

Appear confident
Good posture and eye contact might make you appear more confident. Make
sure your facial expressions are neutral or positive, and avoid making
exaggerated gestures or wringing your hands.

Speak calmly
Assertiveness is not synonymous with confrontation. You express your needs
or concerns clearly. Breathe slowly, and keep your voice steady but calm. If
you're feeling emotional, wait a little before starting the talk.

Consider the emotions and perspectives of others
Nice folks have a lot of empathy. So use it. "I know you're overwhelmed and
stressed, but I can't help you this week."

Consider alternative ideas or make a compromise
Even if you are assertive, you may need to compromise. Be willing to strive
for a solution that is agreeable to everyone involved.

Be brave
You never know how the other person will react when you speak up for
yourself, so you must approach every circumstance with confidence.

Being forceful and nice are not incompatible. Assertiveness allows lovely
people to say what they need to express without becoming angry or resentful

later on. Learn to say "no" while smiling. Ask for what you need from people in a calm and acceptable manner. It will take some practice, but it is a valuable ability to have.

Chapter 4

Understanding People Pleasing

We've learned to compromise and reduce ourselves in order to be loved. The trouble is that when you work so hard to have everyone like you, you frequently end up not loving yourself as much.

Years ago, I greatly wanted everyone to like me. To agree with me and my thoughts. I thought my ability to fit in with different groups of individuals was a desirable trait. Little did I realize, this 'talent' came at a cost. The consequences of not being my actual authentic self. The cost of suppressing my uniqueness.

To be honest, I had to thank this man for helping me recognize I was a people pleaser. It happened a few years ago, and I could tell from our first session that he wanted to be in control and dominate the conversation. Over the course of the sessions, his demands grew. He said that no matter how hard I worked and did my best, there always had to be something more or better I could have done.

And then it occurred to me. During one of our monitored sessions, I recognized I was putting my father's image on him. My lifelong obsession with pleasing my father and gaining his affection and approval has now been projected onto that man. That's because he possessed characteristics that unconsciously reminded me of my father.

Having this knowledge was a game-changer for me. It made me reconsider my relationship patterns and recognize how unhappy I had been for years because I had put so much unwarranted strain on myself to be liked by others. Always satisfy their demands halfway. It was quite taxing. I gradually began to work through these routines and people-pleasing tendencies, eventually breaking free from them.

A people pleaser, according to Merriam-Webster, is someone who has an emotional urge to please others, even if it means sacrificing his or her own needs or desires. A people pleaser will frequently go out of their way to please an individual, even if it means devoting significant time, emotional, or financial resources away from them.

A people pleaser can be a perfectionist, spending a long time rehearsing what they have to say or working diligently on a project that others would not. Constantly trying to please other people can turn into an obsessive habit that becomes their only source of validation since it makes them feel useful and needed. According to the Big 5 Personality Quiz, people-pleasers have greater agreeableness scores.

So the first step is to recognize that you are a people pleaser. The fact that you are reading this book demonstrates that you have become conscious of your people-pleasing behavior. You're not alone. There is nothing wrong with you. This is an aspect you are constantly able to work on and improve. Being a compassionate person who values social relationships and enjoys making other people happy is excellent, but it should not come at the expense of your own happiness and peace of mind.

Where People-pleasing Come From

People-pleasing began in childhood. Perhaps your parents or caretakers gave you conditional love. And by that, I mean that they were either emotionally unavailable or inconsistent in how they expressed love and affection for you.

Parents who believed in harsh affection and would only provide affection and acceptance if you satisfied their ridiculous standards. Or perhaps your parents made you feel unsafe and unprotected, and they may have fought with addiction.

Because youngsters take everything personally, they assume that if they are mistreated, it is because they are not "good enough." Being good as an adult leads individuals to assume, mistakenly, that they have some control in life. They believe that being good will reward them and keep them safe.

People-pleasing is a coping strategy learned in childhood. It is understandable. However, you must understand that it is only a mechanism. Being kind because you believe people would harm you; otherwise, it is a false belief you established over time in the hope of protecting yourself.

Another risk is being involved in violent and poisonous relationships with narcissists and covert abusers who will exploit your niceness. The more you walk on eggshells around them, the more they will detect your desire for love and approval and use it to their advantage.

By taking a sincere look at your relationship patterns, either romantic or platonic, you'll be able to determine if this is the case for you.

Characteristics of people pleasers:

> *Hold yourself in low regard and place others on a pedestal.*
> *I frequently feel like I'm walking on eggshells around other people.*
> *Overexert yourself to meet everyone else's requirements but your own.*
> *Dim yourself to fit in.*
> *If others dislike you, you may believe you have done something wrong or that you are not good enough.*
> *You abandon your own values to meet the needs of others.*
> *Frequently say sorry for trivial things.*
> *Feel responsible for other people's emotions*
> *If you are a people pleaser,*
> *Primarily seek acceptance and validation from outside.*
> *Avoid conflict and debates.*

Women are more prone to be people pleasers. This is due to the long-standing cultural gender roles that women have had to adapt to. Women are educated to be caregivers, with less assertiveness and aggression. How to recognize when your people-pleasing mechanism kicks in:

> *You feel compelled to say no after saying yes.*
> *You don't feel right with the decision you just made.*
> *It seems as though your confidence has diminished.*

If you become aware of these indicators, you will have made enormous progress. That is because you are no longer on autopilot. You are beginning to reclaim your power. It may surprise others at first to see you stand up for yourself. Some others will criticize you, calling you cruel or greedy. But that's because they can't take advantage of you anymore. It will take time for them to get used to the new you, some might even leave you. But, believe me, the correct people will remain in your life and appreciate you for it. Here are the steps to break free from people-pleasing habits:

Take some time to think
This involves taking a somewhat longer delay before responding. If someone presses you to say yes, simply answer: 'I'm busy now, but let me get back to you on that.'

Use 'I don't' instead of 'I can't'
When you are under pressure to do something and begin with 'I can't', those who do not understand boundaries will continue to urge you. Using phrases like 'I don't want to because…' can help establish boundaries and boost confidence.

Do not make assumptions
Make a habit of not forming assumptions. Stop believing it's your fault whenever you notice yourself doing so. Conduct a small investigation. If feasible, ask that person what the problem is. More frequently than not, you'll discover that they had a poor day. Alternatively, something unrelated to you has occurred in their lives.

Keep in mind that you are not accountable for anyone's emotions. You can't make someone feel happy all the time if they don't want to.

If your actions have wronged somebody, chatting about it can easily be repaired. But, as a people pleaser, be wary of getting guilt-tripped. And by that, I mean make sure the other person isn't making you feel bad for something that wasn't your fault only to get something from you.

Know your essential values
Sit down with yourself and jot down your top five life values. For example, if one of your values is a healthy lifestyle but one of your friends is constantly pressuring you to go out and eat junk food or drink excessively, having that value written down makes it simpler for you to say no. If you feel out of sync while responding to someone's request, it's an indication that your people-pleasing behavior has kicked in. And you should question yourself, am I violating my ideals by doing this?

Prioritize what's vital to you
Sit down every week and write down your short-term goals. Additionally, jot out your long-term goals once a month. For example, if you want to take a course to better your abilities, you understand that this is a long-term objective that must be prioritized. Thus, focusing on your education should be at the top of your priority list.

You'll know what to do when someone calls you to interrupt a class to ask for a tiny favor.

Work on increasing your internal validation
Work to boost your self-esteem. Engage in things that are more in line with your soul and avoid putting other people on a pedestal. Yes, looking up to someone is wonderful and encouraging, but continually feeling inferior to others will not help you in any way. Yes, we are social creatures, and it is natural to seek external validation at times, but do not allow it to be your exclusive and primary source of confidence.

You can't please everyone, and that's okay
Despite your best efforts, you will never be able to win over everyone. Be proud of who you are, enjoy each day, and listen to your heart.

There will always be someone who finds something wrong with you or your actions. Or who unconsciously casts their insecurities onto you because you remind them of someone who has wounded them in the past.

Be true to yourself and prioritize your happiness. The more you shine from within, the more it will reflect on the outside. You will meet the ideal folks who will connect with you and be on the same page as you.

Because people-pleasing is an unconscious behavior that you most likely developed in childhood, rebuilding your brain connections to quit is possible, but it will take some time and inner work. It's wonderful to be a giving, caring person, but it's equally crucial to prioritize your own needs by setting appropriate boundaries and concentrating on self-love.

It does not make you selfish; it just makes you understand your own worth. And once you realize your own worth, you will be less ready to make concessions and betray yourself and what you truly believe in.

Chapter 5

Handling Conflict and Disagreement

Disagreements and disagreements are unavoidable, whether in personal or professional relationships. Avoiding unpleasant situations is not the solution; instead, you must handle them with decency and empathy. Here are some powerful concepts for handling conflicts more effectively and amicably.

Recognize people and their perspectives
The first stage in resolving a problem is to acknowledge, accept, and appreciate the other person's point of view. It is crucial to remember that our impression of a situation may not be completely objective, and pushing our point of view may exacerbate the disagreement. Being open to what others perceive and say is critical for successful conflict resolution. This process may be uncomfortable, and that's absolutely fine. It's a learning experience, and you must be gentle to yourself as you try to grasp other people's points of view.

Listen to understand, not respond
Frequently, we listen not so much to understand as to respond. This perspective prevents us from genuinely understanding the other person's point of view since we are preoccupied with planning our own answers. It is critical to fight this impulse and focus solely on what the other person is saying. This approach keeps us on track in the conversation and develops a greater comprehension of the topic at hand.

Ask Mindful and Meaningful Questions
Listening to comprehend should naturally lead to more profound and deliberate inquiries. The goal of these inquiries should not be to prove somebody wrong, but rather to obtain additional information. This method produces a collaborative environment in which both parties work together to reach a solution rather than competing to prove a point. Remember that the nature of the questions we ask can often determine the outcome of an argument.

Work together on the issues
Once you've acknowledged and tried to comprehend other people's points of view, it's time to confront the issue collectively. This phase asks you to see

the other person as a collaborator in resolving the problem rather than an adversary. By being respectful and considerate, you can encourage them to work together to find a solution. This technique is crucial to using kindness and compassion in dispute resolution.

Be open to alternative options
Conflict resolution through kindness and compassion necessitates an openness to other options. You may discover that a blend of different viewpoints provides the greatest solution. Staying stuck in your own perspective can stymie growth and progress, and it is unjust to both persons concerned. Being willing to consider other solutions supports a healthy and productive dispute-resolution process.

Understand the nuances of difficult conversations
Finally, it is critical to comprehend the nuances of unpleasant conversations that occur during confrontations. Sometimes the kindest and most considerate thing to do is to take a break and resume the conversation later. Giving yourself or other people space to reflect can help the discourse. Remember that the goal is not to push too hard, but to keep the discourse flowing. Ultimately, it is about interpreting the circumstance and understanding that each fight has its own reality.

It's not always easy to handle conflicts with kindness and compassion, but it is possible if you practice and commit to these values. Remember to respect other people's points of view, listen to comprehend, ask important questions, collaborate on challenges, be open to alternatives, and understand the complexities of challenging conversations. This will result in not just more successful dispute resolution, but also stronger relationships based on mutual respect and understanding.

Chapter 6

Cultivating Confidence

Self-confidence is more about our belief in ourselves and our skills, which can stem from personal or observed experiences, as well as a belief in our own hard work. A person can be confident in their abilities but dislike themselves as a whole (self-esteem). The sense of self-confidence can be extremely rewarding. Furthermore, research has shown that confidence has a range of benefits. Some of the factors that make confidence crucial are listed below:

Confident individuals are more likely to live longer
A study conducted by Brandeis University in Massachusetts and the University of Rochester in New York discovered that people who are self-confident and persistent are more likely to live longer, healthier lives. According to the study, persons with a strong sense of control and confidence appear to reduce the mortality risk associated with lesser levels of schooling.

Confident individuals are happier
A 2003 study discovered that, with some variance across cultures, people with higher self-esteem were happier, more contented, and had fewer negative mood swings.

Confidence affects both physical and mental wellness
According to research, having high self-esteem has a favorable effect. Confidence is associated with mental health and enjoyment, as well as improved recovery from severe disease.

Confidence is related to success
Although the precise link is unknown, there is frequently a favorable relationship between self-esteem and success. Naturally, rather than confident people being more successful, it's feasible that success increases people's confidence. However, as we discovered when we examined growth mindsets, believing that you can persevere and work hard typically leads to success.

There is a substantial discussion about whether confidence is a talent or a quality. While it may appear that confidence is innate, it is not. Returning to our definition, confidence is comprised of our belief in our potential to succeed and our belief that we can affect events in our lives.

Again, much of this echoes the concept of a growth mentality, which holds that your basic attributes may be developed via effort. So, while IQ and personality are essentially fixed, our confidence in ourselves and our skills can be developed.

Furthermore, we know that there are strategies to increase self-esteem, indicating that it is something we can work on and improve. As a result, it's easy to argue that confidence is a skill. Others think that confidence is an emotion that may be controlled rather than a talent.

A lack of confidence is not always obvious. You may be startled to learn that some of the people you perceive to be self-assured are simply skilled at acting. However, there are other more evident symptoms that someone lacks confidence. Below, we've selected some of the typical indications of a lack of confidence:

Anxiety
Low self-esteem and generalized anxiety disorder are frequently associated. Someone who lacks confidence may appear apprehensive in strange situations. Anxiety can cause us to doubt our talents, and we know that confidence is largely based on belief.

Avoiding challenges
Those who lack confidence are sometimes afraid to try new activities because they do not believe they will succeed.

Avoiding social situations
Meeting new people, including familiar ones, can be difficult when you lack confidence. A lack of confidence in one's social skills frequently leads to avoidance of social situations.

Inadequate self-care
If someone has low self-esteem and confidence in their talents, they may forget to care for themselves. This could include a poor diet, a lack of exercise, or mentally punishing themselves.

Concerned about what others think
People with low self-esteem frequently worry about how others see them. Frequently, people project their own sentiments about themselves onto how they believe others will perceive them.

How To Be Confidence

If you feel like you lack confidence, there are some generally recommended strategies to boost it. Many of these have evidence to back them up, and all have the ability to improve your self-esteem and abilities. Here are our top five methods for increasing confidence:

Practice self-care

Self-confidence and self-care are frequently related. Regular exercise, adequate sleep, and a good diet can all help you feel better about yourself. Taking the time to examine your requirements might help you determine what makes you feel good about yourself. Mindfulness and gratitude practices can also aid with stress reduction, emotion management, and sleep quality.

Create positive relationships

People who are negative and try to knock you down can quickly sap your confidence. Spending less time with those people, as recommended by the NHS, can help you improve your self-esteem. Instead, seek to develop relationships with people who value you. Their positivism can make you feel more assured.

Work on a growth attitude

According to some studies, those with a development mentality have greater levels of self-esteem and resilience than those with a fixed perspective. Although the relationship between confidence and development vs growth mindsets is debatable, cultivating a growth mindset may help you in other areas of your life.

Challenge yourself

To help increase confidence, the NHS recommends creating a task for yourself. Even though it's normal to be afraid to do new things, confident people will take on the challenge. They also propose defining goals, which can aid in the formation of new behaviors, providing focus, and allowing for steady improvement.

Practice self-affirmations

Several research have demonstrated the effectiveness of affirmations. Essentially, talking to yourself about your abilities and confidence will reinforce these positive beliefs. A study discovered that self-affirmations can support us in maintaining our sense of self-efficacy, a crucial element of confidence. Other research has found that when people practice self-affirmation, neuronal networks in their brains respond. Several instances of positive affirmations for confidence are:

> ➤ *I prefer to believe I'm confident.*
> ➤ *I am confident and I cherish myself.*
> ➤ *I am confident about my ability.*
> ➤ *I let go of my limiting thoughts and chose to trust myself.*

It's easy to lack confidence while dealing with others, whether it's speaking with strangers or giving a presentation in front of a large group. However, speaking with confidence is a talent that you can improve. Confidence is an important and valuable characteristic. A lack of confidence can be challenging, but there are ways to overcome it. You can improve your confidence by practicing self-care and self-affirmation, forming strong relationships, challenging yourself, and adopting a growth mindset.

Conclusion

First and foremost, there is nothing wrong with being courteous. It's wonderful to help friends, assist family, and figure out how to get along with others. However, being overly polite can have a variety of undesirable consequences.

Being overly pleasant can just indicate that someone is concerned about disappointing others. The discomfort could be the result of a previous experience with rejection, expressing a viewpoint that was not well accepted, or even having a toxic family history. Whatever happened taught you to constantly say "yes," be nice, and go out of your way to be polite.

The problem is that if your entire life is characterized by being "nice" and doing unselfish things because you're afraid to say no, you can become burnt out and resentful. Being overly kind or not stating your mind will eventually result in deep bitterness. When we are always appeasing others, we can begin to feel invisible, irrelevant, and alienated.

Being extremely kind can result in an identity problem. When you're constantly available to others, you lose track of who you are, what you want, and how you feel. This makes it practically impossible to have honest and vulnerable connections, which are the greatest type. Here are some recommendations for achieving a better balance.

Don't say "sorry."
Try going a full day without saying "sorry." This means that you can't even apologize if someone runs into you. Catching yourself in the present will indicate how frequently you provide excessive apologies, which should help you cut back.

You can also be more assertive in other situations. Instead of apologizing to a friend for being late for lunch, thank them for their patience and waiting for you. Instead of apologizing to your supervisor when you are unable to attend a meeting organized without your involvement, express your gratitude for being included and request a meeting to catch up on the details at a mutually suitable time.

Meet your needs
Try to be more open about your needs. Let your loved ones know that you would appreciate their advice and support. While you're at it, begin prioritizing your own happiness. Don't lose sight of your own needs when assisting

others; instead, strive for a better balance so that you may care for your own well-being.

Do not feel resentful
Practice saying "no" more often, no matter how difficult it is. Reserve all of your attention for things and people who actually mean to you, and you'll be surprised to see how much less burnt out you feel. If you're nervous, text someone and say, "No, I can't do that," then chuck your phone across the room before you're inclined to explain or create an excuse. Doing so will just open the door to negotiation, and guilt may get the best of you. Stick to your guns and respect your schedule.

Don't be concerned about not being liked
Try a thought experiment: Consider circumstances in which you always say yes, and then picture what might happen if you said no. You're probably on autopilot, so finding a method to pause before making a decision helps you stay in control.

From there, look for little scenarios in which you may practice saying no, possibly with little to no danger. If that is too difficult, find someone to practice with. Allow them to participate and have fun with it. For an entire day, let them ask you to do stuff and practice saying no.

Do not get swamped at work
Give yourself permission to set aside time to finish your own chores and goals before considering taking on someone else's. When you're extremely busy, saying no is not only acceptable but also responsible.

Don't get dragged into something you don't want to do
Try to be forceful, even if it is out of character for you. Allow yourself to reject ideas, even if they are unpopular. You cannot expect everyone on the globe to agree with you, therefore don't be hesitant to speak your views.

Don't dismiss your own thoughts
The next time a self-deprecating comment develops in your mouth, swallow it. Knocking yourself down is a habit that can only be broken by doing the opposite.

Don't back out of plans
If you have a propensity to answer yes too rapidly, practice postponing your reaction. Say something like, "Oh, you know what? After giving it some thought, I'll get back to you in an hour. I want to make sure I can say yes

without any other conflicts, or decline with enough time to see if anyone else
is available. In that method, you honor your own feelings while also
respecting the time and feelings of the person asking for something.
Remember that someone would prefer an honest and timely 'no' over a
dishonest and obligatory 'sure!'

Don't allow people say rude things to you
Set appropriate boundaries with others. Correct anyone who attempts to
degrade you or breaks the boundaries you've established in your relationship
with them. It may take time for them to adjust but remain firm.

Express yourself
Understand that discussing your ideas is neither mean nor incorrect. People
will feel closer to you if you are honest about your emotions, so consider
opening up a little. The next time you're angry, don't grin on the surface while
you rage on the inside. Instead, respond, "You know what? "I'm not okay with
that."

It may even be useful to consult with a therapist. People can be overly nice
when there are penalties for acting differently as children. If your parents
taught you that it is unacceptable to express your feelings, it may be good to
retrain how to act. With coaching, you'll see that being "nice" isn't the only
proper emotion.

Do not tire yourself
Remember that being "nice" is not the same as being genuinely kind.
Whereas niceness could be a reluctance to say 'no' or defer to others,
kindness can take the shape of loving confrontation or allowing the people in
your life to suffer the consequences of activities that are damaging to you.
The more you speak up and care for yourself, the less exhausted you will
feel.

Don't dodge confrontation
Practice being aggressive, even if the word makes your blood run cold. It's
not as difficult as it appears, especially since being assertive does not require
you to be unpleasant or disrespectful. It only requires you to advocate for
yourself. This is something you can do gradually in your ordinary life or with
the help of a therapist.

Avoid attracting "Needy" people
The next time someone wants to drag you into their drama, take a step back
and ask yourself if you have the time and energy to help. If not, clearly state

your boundaries. Something like "It means a lot that you trust me with this information, but I can't talk about it right now" will suffice.

If you're used to being overly kind, it will take time to replace the habit and all of the attendant stress with something healthier, but it is feasible. Remember that being pleasant is not the same as being kind. Kindness is wonderful, so strive for it instead.